First Dates

The Stines' Super Survival Kit #1

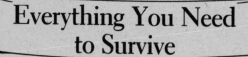

Everything You Need to Survive

First Dates

By Jane Stine and Jovial Bob Stine

Illustrated by Sal Murdocca

RANDOM HOUSE NEW YORK

Library of Congress Cataloging in Publication Data:
Stine, Jane. Everything you need to survive first dates.
  (The Stines' super survival kit ; #1)
  SUMMARY: A guide to coping with the first date, including advice on places to go, commonsense etiquette, conversation, clothes, and things to do. Text is interspersed with a selection of jokes and humorous anecdotes.
  1. Dating (Social customs)—Juvenile literature. [1. Dating (Social customs)—Handbooks, manuals, etc. 2. Handbooks, manuals, etc.] I. Stine, Jovial Bob. II. Murdocca, Sal, ill. III. Title. IV. Series: Stine, Jane. Stines' super survival kit ; #1.
  HQ801.S83   1983   646.7'7   82-24045   ISBN: 0-394-85246-X

Manufactured in the United States of America   1 2 3 4 5 6 7 8 9 0

Inside This Super Survival Kit

Introduction:
Identify the Problem

You Know It's Going to Be a Long Evening When...

Before you and your date can get out the door, your mother brings out sixteen photo albums to show him what you looked like as a baby!

Her father is a gym teacher, and while you're waiting for her to come downstairs, he forces you into a contest to see who can do the most situps and pushups!

Before you pick her up, you have a huge dinner at home of spaghetti and meatballs, chili, cheesecake, and chocolate fudge ripple ice cream. Then she greets you at her door with "Where are we going for dinner?"

He keeps calling you Alice, and your name is Bernice!

He keeps asking if you know what's on TV at nine!

You compliment him on his shirt, and he insists on describing to you in detail every article of clothing in his closet!

He says "Hi, howya doin' " three or four times, and then can't think of anything else to say!

She asks if her aunt Eldred can come along to the party because "the poor old dear doesn't get out much these days"!

He brings his sea shell collection along to the dance because he has so many interesting stories to share with you about them!

At the movie theater he counts how many kernels you have in your box of popcorn to make sure you didn't get more than he did!

She takes out her knitting as soon as you arrive at the dance and tells you she wants to finish the whole sweater before it's time to go home!

He keeps throwing his head back and laughing at the top of his lungs for no reason at all!

She keeps asking if you'd like to sing "Twinkle, Twinkle, Little Star" as a two-part round!

You've only been together for half an hour and he's telling you the same joke for the fourth time!

Let's face it. Dates are not always like in the movies—unless the movies you go to are horror shows! And first dates are usually creep shows for just about everyone.

What to wear . . . what to say . . . what not to say . . . what to do . . . when to laugh . . . when to try and be serious—there are just too many things to think about to ever really relax and have a good time.

But wait. Don't spend next Saturday night in your room picking fleas off the dog just to avoid a bad date. This *Super Survival Kit* is filled with first aid for first dates. Here are some answers to your biggest dating problems—and lots of laughs to make your biggest problems seem a little smaller.

It's all here: places to go, questions to ask, ways to break the ice, commonsense etiquette to remember—plus humor, jokes, and funny stuff to help make even the *longest* evening seem just a bit shorter!

Is *This* How to Ask for a Date? Don't Ask!

When it comes to asking someone new for a date, most people would rather have a few teeth pulled or take a six-hour geography test (all essay questions). This is because it can be a little embarrassing to ask for a date.

Now, your *Super Survival Kit* almost comes to your rescue with these examples of incorrect and correct ways to ask for a date. These examples won't help make it any easier to ask someone out—but at least they will give you a few laughs while you're working up the courage to make that all-important phone call to that lucky someone!

Incorrect: "Hello (haha). You don't know me (ha ha hee hee giggle). But then again, I don't know you either (hahahaha heeheeheehee giggle giggle ha ha). How about a date?"

Correct: "Hello (sophisticated chuckle). You don't know me (suave chortle). But then again, I don't know you, either (polite guffaw). How about a date?"

Incorrect: "Hello, you don't know me, but I'm a friend of your cousin Al from Des Moines, and he told me you were desperate to go out on a date, so I thought I'd give you a break and call to ask you out."

Correct: "Hello. Allow me to introduce myself. My name is _____ . I'm a friend of your cousin Al from Des Moines. He told me you were desperate to go out on a date, so I thought I'd give you a break and call to ask you out."

Incorrect: "My friend bet me ten dollars that you wouldn't go out with me next Saturday. Please help me win the bet."

Correct: "My friend bet me ten dollars that you wouldn't go out with me next Saturday. Please help me win the bet, and I'll split the money with you fifty-fifty."

Incorrect: "Everyone else I called said no, so I thought I'd call you and see if you'd go to the dance with me."

Correct: "Everyone else I called said no, so I thought I'd call you and see if you'd go to the dance with me—*please*."

Incorrect: "Give me two good reasons why you can't go out with me Friday night."

Correct: "Give me *ten* good reasons why you can't go out with me Friday night!"

Incorrect: "I—uh—well—I mean—uh, er— well . . . you know."

Correct: "I—uh—well—I mean—uh, er— well . . . you know—er—Saturday night?"

Incorrect: "A bunch of us are going down to the arcade to play some video games. I thought maybe you'd like to come along with me."

Correct: "A bunch of us are going down to the arcade to play some video games. I thought maybe you'd like to come along with me—and bring several rolls of quarters!"

Incorrect: "Whatcha doin' Friday night, Baby Face?"

Correct: "What are you doing Friday night, Baby Face?"

Incorrect: "Hi, you don't probably not want to not go to the movies with me, don't you?"

Correct: (Sorry. We're still trying to figure out the *incorrect* one!)

Even with these helpful suggestions, asking someone out for a date isn't always easy. In fact, you might find it less painful to ask someone out for a *non*date! For some no-nonsense nondate suggestions, keep reading.

Take a Date on a Nondate Date

Everyone knows what a first date is, right? Nervousness, awkwardness, uncomfortable clothes, etiquette, small talk—yuck! We're breaking out in hives just thinking about it!

Maybe first dates *used* to be like that, but they don't have to be anymore. A first date doesn't have to be a formal ritual. It should just be a way to spend some time with someone, get to know him or her a little better, and have some fun. Yes, we said *fun*.

First dates *can* be fun—especially if they're nondate dates like these.

The Movie Nondate Date

Here's a new kind of movie date that's bound to make you a star. Instead of going to the movies on a date (how common!), do what the movie stars do—have a private screening.

Pick a night when there's a really good movie on cable or regular TV, and invite some friends (including the person you're especially interested in) to your personal screening room. If you're lucky enough to have a video recorder (or if you know someone who has one) get a group of kids together and chip in to rent a movie on tape. With three or more kids, it's much cheaper than actually going to the movies, believe it or not!

Pop a bunch of popcorn, arrange the chairs in the TV room in rows, and let the show begin.

Remember—a bad movie may be even more fun than a good one. And the bigger the crowd, the better the laughs!

The Member-Bring-a-Nonmember
Nondate Date

If you belong to a club, or team, or any group that meets fairly regularly, you've got a great way of getting together with the opposite sex—without having a nervous breakdown in the process.

Simply ask each member of your group to bring someone of the opposite sex to your next get-together. But be sure to make it clear that this is *not* a date—it is a chance to participate in the group's activity.

For example, if you have an all-male Dungeons & Dragons™ game every Thursday night, invite some girls for next Thursday who would like to learn how to play. Or let some boys join your girls' softball team for a game or two.

This is a good solution to the "I don't know how to ask him/her" problem, since you can phrase your invitation in terms of the activity—not as a date date. "Gee, would you like to see Roger's new TSR Eighty? Our computer club is having an open session, and I know you are interested in computers, so. . . ." This kind of invitation is much easier to deal with than "Do you want to go out with me Friday night?"

Try it—it works!

The Nonpicnic Nondate Date

Here's an idea that's so dumb it just might be brilliant. Invite some friends or just one special friend to a picnic—in the middle of winter.

Don't worry about frostbite. This is a nonpicnic picnic—you'll have it indoors! You can have the traditional sandwiches, deviled eggs, lemonade—the works. Just spread a blanket on the floor of your basement, family room, or your own room, and dig in!

Who could refuse a creative idea like this one? And with any luck the ants won't show up till spring!

The Ice Cream Olympics Nondate Date

A date has a much better chance of being successful if the participants have something in common. Well, one thing that almost everyone has in common is a love of ice cream. Now, this may not sound like enough to build a longstanding relationship on—but it's not a bad place to start.

With that in mind, why not have an Ice Cream Olympics? Get a group of kids together and go ice-creaming out of your minds!

Chip in and buy all of the fancy new brands of ice cream and have a taste test. Set out a table of nuts, candies, syrups, and toppings and have the world's most incredible sundae competition.

Take notes, give prizes, keep busy. You may not even notice that you've been on a date—until your stomachache goes away the next day!

The School Project Nondate Date

Have you got the kind of teacher who likes to assign projects where you have to go to a museum, or look something up in the city clerk's office, or go down to the public library (since the school library's files don't go back *that* far)? We know the type. And we also know that these study projects can come in very handy in the nondate department.

A school project is the perfect excuse for a nondate date. Ask that special him or her in your class to work with you, and you'll have half the work and double the fun.

This is a real no-stress situation because your time together has a real purpose. There'll be no need for small talk, since you'll be talking about how you should divide the work, where you should start, how you should proceed, and so on. This is an A+ idea—really!

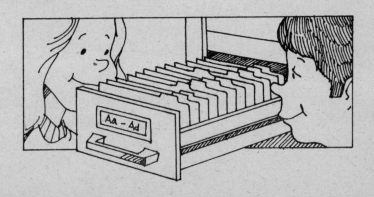

The Girls vs. Boys Video Games
Nondate Date

Whether at the home game console or the local arcade, a video game can be a great equalizer. Get a group of boys and girls together and find out which is the quickest sex.

Don't let the competition get *too* fierce, though. The idea is to come out of this friends—not foes!

23

The Shopping Nondate Date

You know the old saying: When the going gets tough, the tough go shopping. But you'll find that there's nothing tough about asking someone of the opposite sex to go shopping with you.

Christmas is the ideal time for this nondate, when everybody has to go shopping for gifts. Just think how useful it would be to have a girl along with you when you have to pick out a gift for your sister.

And think how much more bearable the wait at the cash register will be if there's someone interesting to talk to. No question about it, this idea is a real bargain!

Practice Your Dating Conversation

There's nothing like *talking* to keep a conversation going. And when you talk to your date, you want to be impressive, funny, and smart. Being a good talker doesn't come naturally. You need practice, practice, practice. Here's a way to practice your dating conversation skills—without appearing to be talking to yourself!

In this chapter we've provided you with all of the conversation for an entire date. Everything your date says to you is right here on the page. We've put blanks in the places where *you* do the talking.

As you will soon see, this date requires some fast thinking—and some fast talking on your part. Good luck. And remember—this is only practice. When you're out on a real date, don't wait for blanks to appear before you start talking!

"Hi. How come you were so late?"

_____

_____

"Oh, come on! Stop joking! What was the *real* reason?"

_____

_____

"Well, don't worry about it. We still have time to make the movie. What movie are we seeing?"

_____

_____

"Oh, really? I've seen it twice. But maybe it'll be better the third time. How do you feel about movies like this one where it's the detective himself who committed the crime?"

_____

_____

"Well, I hope I didn't spoil it for you by giving away the ending. Hey—what an unusual shirt you're wearing. I don't think I've ever seen that shade of green on a human being before. How would you describe it?"

_____

_____

"Well, we'll be sitting in the dark so maybe people won't notice it too much. Do you know what's green just like your shirt, has sixteen legs, and bites?"

_____

_____

"I don't either—but it's crawling up your neck! Ha ha ha ha! Now you tell me one! Go ahead— I love jokes!"

_____

_____

_____

(Yawn) "Sorry. I've heard that one before. Tell me another one. Come on—hurry."

_____

_____

_____

"I'm pretty sure I've heard that one too. You know, you look different from the last time I saw you. Shorter, or something. What's different about you?"

_____

_____

"Well, have you been seeing a doctor about it?"

_____

_____

"And what on earth have you done to your hair?"

_____

_____

"Oh, really? Well, don't worry. It'll grow back in a year or two. Can I ask you a really important question?"

_____

"Gee . . . I forget what I was going to ask. Why don't you ask me a really important question instead. I love important questions. Go ahead—ask me one."

_____

_____

"Wow. That's a good one. I'll have to give that one some thought. You're real deep, you know. Hey—someone told me that you have an unusual hobby that involves snorkeling for garbage. Would you like to tell me about it?"

_____

_____

_____

"Well, now I've heard just about everything! Ha ha! That's too much. Someone told me you also do interesting things with raisins. What do you do with raisins? Tell me!"

_____

_____

"You're weird. You're definitely weird. What's the weirdest thing you've ever done?"

_____

_____

"You really think that's so weird? I do that twice a week! Hey—what's that package all gift-wrapped there? Is that a surprise for me?"

_____

_____

"Gee, you shouldn't have. Especially since I already have six of them. But don't feel bad. It's the thought that counts. Let me ask you a question: What do you think is the meaning of life? I'm serious. Hey—where are you going? What? You're taking me home? But what about the movie? What about our date? Why are you doing this?"

_____

_____

Don't Say It!

Silence. An awkward pause in the conversation. You had a hundred things you wanted to say to your date—and now you can't think of a single one. You stare at the ceiling for a while, then you look down at your shoes. What should you do?

Our advice is to BE CAREFUL. In desperate moments like this, when the silence is so loud it's deafening, you may find yourself saying exactly the wrong thing. Before you speak, pull out your *Super Survival Kit* and go over this handy list. After all, you want to get the *conversation* moving—you don't want to get your *date* moving out the door!

Thirty Things Not to Say—Even When You Can't Think of Anything Else!

1. You're not half as boring as you used to be.

2. How many diseases can you think of?

3. I've had my braces off for exactly six months, three weeks, two days, and eight hours. How about you?

4. You're not really cross-eyed. You just look as if you are.

5. I enjoy these quiet moments when we're both pretending we don't notice how quiet it is, don't you?

6. What in your opinion is the meaning of life?

7. You're not half as silly as people say.

8. That's a pretty dress. My grandmother has one just like it.

9. I can make forty-five funny noises with my lips and tongue. Would you like to hear them?

THAT'S NOT WHAT I MEANT.

10. Let me give you some good advice.

11. How do we know we are really sitting here in this room and not just figments of someone's imagination?

12. How many cities can you think of that begin with the letter Q?

13. I know some fascinating facts about the African bull elephant. For one thing, they're a lot bigger than you probably think.

14. I'd offer you some gum if I had any.

15. I really like that dress. And I liked it when you wore it last year, and the year before that.

16. Gee, from across the room I could barely

see that bright red rash on your neck.

17. When was the last time your skin turned blue?

18. You have a great sense of humor. We all laugh our heads off the minute you enter a room.

19. I feel so much at home here in your house. I guess it's because I used to spend a lot of time hanging around the junkyard.

20. Don't worry. You hair will grow back in two or three years.

21. Do you think it's a coincidence that I have ingrown toenails on both feet?

22. I'll bet I can sneeze farther than you can.

23. It's weird how much your dog looks like you.

24. You're probably wondering how I got the nickname Salami Breath!

25. There are thirty-eight different kinds of bacteria that can infect your throat. Let me explain.

26. How do you think they fit all those sardines into those tiny little cans?

27. You're probably wondering how I keep my shirt cuffs from wrinkling.

28. I really respect my elders, don't you?

29. I'll bet that twenty or thirty years from now we'll think back to this night, and we won't be able to remember it at all.

30. What do you think of me so far?

A Silence Solution—
Jokes to Tell

Those long silences seem to be getting longer? That's no joke. Here's a *Super Survival Kit* solution—a few lonnnnnnnng jokes to tell to make the hours seem shorter. We think any date will seem *too* short—if it's long on laughs!

A baseball team had spent the last three years in last place. The manager was desperate. He was ready to try anything to start winning ballgames.

One day a horse walked into his office. "I want to play on your team," the horse said.

The manager was a little surprised. No major league baseball team had ever had a horse for a player. But finally the manager said, "Why not? I don't have anything to lose."

The next day the manager sent the horse out to the mound to be the starting pitcher. In the first inning the horse struck out all three batters. In the second and third innings the horse struck out all three batters.

In the bottom of the third the horse came up to bat. He hit the first pitch deep into right field. It missed going over the fence by inches. The right fielder couldn't believe his eyes. He fielded the ball on the first bounce and threw it to the shortstop. The shortstop dropped the ball, picked it up, then threw it to first. The throw was wild. The second baseman chased it, picked it up, and threw it to first. The ball got there way before the horse did, and he was out at first base.

The horse went back to the dugout. "You know," said the manager, "you're a terrific pitcher. And you can really hit that ball. But you're the slowest runner I've ever seen in my life."

"If I could run," the horse said, "do you think I'd be here?"

It was a beautiful spring day in the city. The sky was filled with pigeons flying happily in the warm breeze. Two of the pigeons nearly crashed into each other.

"Hey—watch where you're going!" the female pigeon yelled. "You scraped my wing, you clod!"

"Gee, I'm sorry," the embarrassed male pigeon said. "It's just that you're so beautiful, I couldn't take my eyes off you, and I forgot what I was doing."

"Why, thank you," the female pigeon said, her angry tone disappearing.

"Will you join me here for lunch tomorrow?" the male pigeon asked.

"I'd be happy to," she said. "I'll see you tomorrow at noon." Then she flew off.

Every day after that the two pigeons met to have lunch together. After a week had gone by, the male pigeon said, "I'm getting tired of this spot. Why don't we meet at the waterfront tomorrow?"

"Fine," she replied. "I'll bring the sandwiches."

Their lunch date was for noon. He got there early and waited on the window ledge of a building. She wasn't there at noon. Half an hour later he was still waiting for her. He began to pace back and forth on the ledge.

By one o'clock he was a nervous wreck. "I can't imagine what's keeping her," he said to himself. "I hope she isn't sick."

Just then he looked down at the sidewalk, and there she was. He flew down to her. "Thank goodness you're safe," he said. "I've been so worried about you. What happened?"

"Nothing," she said. "It was such a lovely day, I decided to walk."

A young writer decided he wanted to write for the movies. So he sat down and wrote an 800-page comedy script. He flew out to Hollywood and took his script to a movie producer.

"I'm sorry," the producer said. "We've had too many comedies."

So the young man flew home and tried to think of something else to write. He got an idea for a mystery, and he wrote a long script. Then he took some more money out of his savings account, flew to Hollywood, and took his script to the producer.

"I'm sorry," the producer said. "We've had too many mysteries."

The young man was not discouraged. He flew home and the next day he began work on a love story. He worked on the script for two years. When it was finally finished, he flew to Hollywood and took it to the movie producer.

"I'm sorry," the producer said. "We've had too many love stories."

The writer flew home and tried and tried to think of something that hadn't been done before. Finally he wrote a script about a talking dog.

He took out his last remaining dollars, flew to Hollywood, and took his script to the producer. "This dog," he told the producer, "is the most talented animal that ever lived. He can talk in thirty-two languages, play the piano, run a mile in a minute, throw a football a hundred yards, and sing opera."

"Wonderful!" screamed the producer. "We could make a fortune on this one. This dog sounds great. What kind of a dog is he?"

"A boxer," said the writer.

"No good," said the producer. "We've had too many fight pictures!"

Three kids were sitting around the house one day trying to figure out what to do. "We could toss around a football," said Eddie, the oldest.

"Yeah—if we had a football," said Freddie, the youngest.

"And if we wanted to toss around a football, which I *don't*!" said Susan, who wasn't the oldest or the youngest.

"We could play hide and seek," suggested Freddie.

"That's too babyish," said Eddie.

"We could build a tree house," suggested Susan.

"That's too hard," said Freddie.

"And we don't have any lumber," said Eddie.

"And come to think of it, we don't have a tree," said Susan.

"We could ride our bikes," said Eddie.

"We did that yesterday," said Susan.

"Wait a minute! Wait a minute!" cried Eddie. "We don't even know if it's nice outside. Maybe the weather is terrible and we should be thinking of indoor things to do instead of outdoor things."

"That's very smart," said Susan. "One of us should check the weather and then we'll know what to plan. One of us should go take a look out the window."

"I went last time," said Eddie, refusing to budge from his comfortable spot on the floor.

"I'll go next time," said Susan, also refusing to move. "I guess you're elected, Freddie."

So Freddie slowly pulled himself up to his feet and walked over to the window. A few seconds later he came back.

"Well?" Susan asked. "What's the weather?"

"I don't know," said Freddie.

"You *must* know what the weather is like," said Eddie. "You looked out the window, didn't you?"

"Yes, I did," said Freddie. "But it's raining so hard I couldn't tell!"

Test Your Dating Etiquette

How prepared are you for those unexpected, difficult situations that crop up on almost every date? Do you know the polite thing to say when your date's hand gets caught in a refrigerator door? The polite thing to do after you've accidentally blown up your date's car?

Take this test to check your knowledge of dating etiquette. Simply circle the correct answer to each question. Then check your results at the end of the test.

1. You're having dinner at your girlfriend's house, and her mother serves liver, your least favorite dish. You should:

   a. politely excuse yourself and run home.

   b. pretend to take big bites out of it with an invisible fork. This way, they'll think you're crazy, and her mom won't be insulted if you don't eat.

   c. toss it across the room, saying, "My, that's the lightest liver I've ever seen. I *must* have the recipe!"

2. You're having dinner at your girlfriend's house, and the table is set very formally. You don't know which fork to use to eat your salad. You should:

   a. politely excuse yourself and run home.

   b. use two or three forks at once to make sure you're using the correct one.

   c. yell, "Hey—what's that up on the ceiling?" And when everyone looks up, gobble down your salad as fast as you can.

3. You're supposed to meet your boyfriend at the school dance. But he's already more than an hour late. You should:

 a. go in and start dancing by yourself till he arrives.

 b. go to a phone and call yourself so you'll have someone to talk to while you're waiting.

 c. go home and tear the fur off your dog till you're not feeling angry anymore.

4. Your boyfriend finally shows up an hour and a half late, and he apologizes by saying, "Sorry, I got hung up." You should:

    a. go and tear the fur off your boyfriend's dog till you're not feeling angry anymore.

    b. say nonchalantly, "Oh, are you late? I was having such a good time, I didn't notice!"

    c. tell him that after he takes you to the dance and then out for a bite to eat, you're never going to speak to him again.

5. Everyone else at the party is in jeans and T-shirts, and you made the dreadful mistake of getting all dressed up. You should:

    a. explain that you thought it was a "come-as-you-are party" and this is the way you always dress around your house.

    b. tell everyone you thought it was supposed to be a costume party, and how embarrassing it must be for them to have all chosen the same costume!

    c. flap your arms, run around in circles, and cluck like a chicken. Everyone thinks you're a weirdo anyway. You might as well make the most of it!

6. In the middle of the school dance your girl-friend says, "I'm sorry, but I'm really not feeling well. I think I'm sick." You should:

    a. say, "Thank goodness! At least there's a good reason for why you look so terrible!"

    b. say, "Why tell *me* about it? I'm not a doctor!" and keep trying to dance with her as best as you can.

    c. slip a surgical mask over your face just in case what she has is contagious.

7. You're standing at your front door and your date wants to kiss you good night, but you really don't want to. You should:

   a. toss a large, juicy plug of chewing tobacco into your mouth and hope he'll take the hint.

   b. say, "I'm sorry, but I have to save my lips for my tuba lesson first thing tomorrow morning."

   c. hold the back of your hand up to your lips and make loud kissing noises on it. Then, as your date runs off in disgust, you say, "You mean this isn't how it's done?"

Check Your Results

Don't you know it's extremely rude to be taking ridiculous tests when you should be out making friends and working on your social life? Shame on you! We're so disappointed in you, we're not even going to tell you how you did on the test.

But seriously, folks, you'd never know it from this test, but dating etiquette—knowing *what* to do *when* in social situations—is a real problem for everyone who is starting to date.

Our next Super Survival chapter should help answer some of the serious questions we all have at one time or another. Keep reading.

Help Yourself to Some Super Survival Etiquette

Most kids think etiquette is a bunch of do's and don'ts designed to make you feel nervous and uncomfortable about the way you're acting. In fact, etiquette is supposed to be just the opposite.

The so-called rules of etiquette aren't really rules. They are guidelines to help you feel *more* comfortable. Think about it—if you're in a strange situation, and you've been *told* exactly what you're expected to do, you're going to be more at ease than if you're trying to guess what to do by looking around the room and seeing what others are doing.

The problem with kids and etiquette is that many of the "rules" of etiquette are simply old-fashioned, or not relevant to kids, or too unnatural. (It's just *dumb* for a boy to have to open a door for a girl when they're each carrying a forty-pound backpack!)

What's needed here is realistic, sensible help, not outdated attitudes. So stay tuned as we answer your questions about dating etiquette.

Let's start with the biggie—money!

Question: Does a boy have to pay for everything on a date?

Super Survival Etiquette: Of course not! The idea behind paying for a date is fine—it's just a way of showing people that you care about them and want them to have a nice time. But the reality is expensive and also shows an old-fashioned attitude toward girls.

Boys, there is nothing wrong with asking a girl to pay for her movie ticket—especially if you're honest about it up front. You can say, "I'd really like to see *Revenge of the Red Herrings* with you Saturday afternoon, but I'm a little low on money. Would you mind paying for your own ticket?"

Or try a subtler approach: "Would you like to go see the Red Flame concert at the arena? The tickets go on sale at noon. Why don't we go down and buy tickets together?"

This is perfectly acceptable behavior—really. But it can be difficult to pull off. In some ways it's easier for the girl to take the initiative in the money department.

Girls, there's nothing wrong with saying, "Sure, I'd like to go to the movies—but let me pay for my ticket." Or: "You paid for the movie last time. Let me pay this time." Or even: "You paid for the movie. Let me pay for the ice cream afterward."

Or if that's too difficult, try: "Gee, you already spent ten bucks on the movie. Why don't we skip the restaurant and go home to my house and make sundaes there?"

Money is always a touchy subject, but you can handle it—honest.

Question: Is it okay for a girl to ask a boy out?

Super Survival Etiquette: Of course it's okay. Many girls feel uncomfortable about doing it. But here's something for you girls to remember—boys also feel uncomfortable about asking girls out!

It's hard to put yourself on the line, no matter which gender you are. But it can be made a little easier. Try one of the Super Survival Nondate dates you'll find elsewhere in this kit. They make the whole process easier for boys *and* girls.

Another tip to ease the tension is to focus your invitation on the activity rather than on yourself.

For example: "I've got two tickets for the soccer final Friday night. Would you like to go?"

Remember, asking for a date may be tough. But once you've done it, you never have to do it for the first time again!

Question: What about all that opening doors, carrying bags, pulling out chairs stuff? Do boys really have to do that? Do girls really have to wait for them to do it?

Super Survival Etiquette: The answer here is, use your common sense. If you're a 6-foot-tall weight lifter and she's a 98-pound weakling, it's probably sensible and kind if you carry her 20-pound science project.

The good idea behind all this door-opening stuff is to show someone you have concern for him or her. You can do that by being helpful when the situation calls for it—and that goes for girls and boys.

When a door opens in toward you, it's sensible to open it and let the other person go through first. When it pushes out, it's easier to go through first and hold the door from the inside. And the person who does the pushing and pulling should be the person who gets there first!

Question: Does a boy always have to pick a girl up for a date? And what about seeing her home from the date?

Super Survival Etiquette: Practicality is the answer here. There's nothing wrong with meeting at the movies, especially if you and your date live miles away from each other.

But here are a few things to keep in mind:

1. Parents generally like to meet their kids' friends and dates. They may be a bit old-fashioned about this. And it isn't smart to get your parents or your date's parents worried, upset, or annoyed.

2. If you're walking to the movies, or to a dance, or wherever, it is safer (and more pleasant) to walk with someone.

Since most of you are too young to drive, picking up a date usually means having your parents drive you. This may be somewhat embarrassing—but it certainly beats walking for miles! Incidentally, there's nothing wrong with a girl and her parents picking up the boy—especially if it's more convenient for her parents to drive than for his.

Question: How do you know what to wear on a date?

Super Survival Etiquette: These days, luckily, the conventions of fashion are pretty loose. When it comes to clothes, just about anything goes. But here are a few suggestions:

1. Don't get very dressed up for a first date. The reason for this is common sense: First dates are a bit nerveracking, and you'll tend to be even more tense if you're dolled up in fancy clothes.

The best rule of thumb is to wear something you would wear to school on a day when you wanted to look especially good. Save the gold lamé jumpsuit for when you know each other a little better!

2. Ties are hardly ever required for boys anymore. But if you're going out to dinner at a fancy restaurant with your girlfriend and her parents, you can call the restaurant and check. Whoever answers the phone will be glad to tell you the dress code.

The same goes for girls. There are still some restaurants that don't allow women in slacks. Call and check.

3. Know your audience. That means your new

punk outfit might be a big hit with your friends, but it might give your friends' parents the shakes! Of course, it's stupid to judge people by their clothes—but most people cannot help doing it to a certain extent. For that reason, it makes sense to try to figure out the impression you may be making with your clothes and decide whether that's the impression you want to make.

4. Girls don't have to wear flat shoes if they are taller than their dates. In this day and age there are a lot more important things than height!

Question: Do you really have to call a week in advance for a date? Is it rude to ask at the last minute?

Super Survival Etiquette: No, you don't have to ask for a date a week in advance. But common sense will tell you that your chances of getting a "yes" are better if you give your date some notice.

If something comes up at the last moment, however, there's nothing wrong with asking then. And no one should ever be so old-fashioned as to turn down an invitation just because it came at the last moment. That's dumb!

Question: What about kissing?

Super Survival Etiquette: Oh, go ahead! Don't worry about where the noses go. Nobody kisses like in the movies. But it *always* works out okay. And you *don't* have to kiss someone just because he or she has gone out with you. In fact, you don't have to kiss anyone if you don't want to!

As you can see, our Super Survival Etiquette is pretty relaxed about most things. But nonetheless there are a few do's and don'ts worth remembering. . . .

DON'T leave your date stranded to go off and talk with your other friends.

DON'T spend a whole date talking about yourself and not asking about your date.

DO offer to pitch in and help with the dishes and so on if you're having dinner at your date's home.

DON'T demand that everything be done your way on a date. Talk about alternative plans and decide together what you want to do.

DON'T ever bring a friend along on a date unless your date knows about it and agrees to it in advance.

DON'T brag! Bragging is bad manners and turns people off faster than anything.

DO be pleasant and kind even if after ten minutes you know you never want to go out with this person again.

Etiquette Rules of the Past

You think it's tough to know the rules of etiquette today? What about thirty, forty, or fifty years ago when there *really were* etiquette rules? Young people back then had a lot more to worry about than which T-shirt would be most appropriate to wear to the dance!

For example, here are some real etiquette rules we found in books, rules your parents and grandparents probably read when they were about your age.

"A young lady should never dine in a restaurant with a boy unless accompanied by a chaperone."

"Boys should never wear fedora hats, jewelry, or silk socks to a party or dance."

"Young girls may not go to the movies in the afternoon without an older person—unless the town is so small that the theater employees know who the girls are."

"A young man should always dance with the two young ladies who sat beside him at dinner. It is an attractive thing to do because it shows the young ladies that he liked them."

"Never say, 'I partook of liquid refreshment.' Always say instead, 'I had something to drink.'"

"A young woman should never eat candy at the theater or in any public place."

"Young women are not allowed to go to prize-fights with a boy, or with a group of girls and boys."

"When a girl must pay a long visit to the dentist's office, she should be accompanied by her mother, an aunt or other relative, or her maid."

"Young men should remove their white gloves when eating dinner, unless they are only eating a cup of soup."

"Girls of eleven and twelve are not allowed to meet boys at the corner drugstore for a soda. Girls of this age are not allowed to walk on the streets of a big city alone, except to and from a bus stop."

"A young man always waits to call a young lady by her first name until she gives permission to do so. A young lady may say, '*Please*, don't call me Miss Benson. Call me Alice.' Or she may simply begin calling the boy by his first name. But under no circumstances should a young man offer first by saying, '*Do* call me Henry.' "

Break the Ice

Okay, so you've followed our advice and you've invited some kids over (including that special someone). And now all the boys are standing on one side of the room, and all the girls are on the other. Hey—you've got to get this party moving! Have no fear. Your *Super Survival Kit* is here with some handy Ice Breakers.

Ice Breakers are games that force people at a party to get together. Sure they're corny, slightly embarrassing, and they make you feel dumb. That's just the point! How can you feel embarrassed and awkward at a party when everyone else in the room is acting and feeling like a jerk? We rest our case.

Ice Breaker #1: Backward Fun

Before the party write the name of each guest on a separate slip of paper. After everyone has arrived, pin a name on each person's back. Now, here's the embarrassing part: Pin girls' names on boys' backs and boys' names on girls' backs.

The object of the game (of course) is to guess whose name is on your back. To do this, each guest can ask yes or no questions of all the other guests. (No fair asking about clothes, though. That makes it too easy.)

Once a guest has guessed the name correctly, he or she must go to that person to confirm the guess. This way everyone gets paired off—at least for a little while.

Ice Breaker #2: Beep Bop!

This one is really dumb—but at least it's good and noisy. Here's how it goes:

Everyone stands in a circle with the host (you) in the middle. You turn around and around and point to someone in the circle. As you point you yell, "One, two, three, four, five, BEEP!"

If you point with your left hand, the person you point to must yell out the name of the person on his or her left and then yell "BOP!" *before* you say "BEEP!"

If you point with your right hand, the person must yell the name of the person on his or her right and add "BOP!" before you yell "BEEP!" If you get to "BEEP" first, the person you pointed to is "it" and comes into the center of the circle, and you start again.

Keep it up for ten minutes or so, until everybody is giggling, or threatening to burn your house down—whichever comes first!

Ice Breaker #3: Ha Ha

This one is so embarrassing, it should be rated R for Ridiculous. Here's what you do:

You lie down on the floor face up. Then someone else lies down face up with his or her head resting on your stomach. Then the next person lies down face up with his or her head resting on the second person's stomach. Keep going until you're all lying in a big circle and everyone has a stomach to rest his or her head on.

Now, the first person (that's you) says "Ha."
The second person says "Ha ha." The third person
says "Ha ha ha"—and so on.

Keep going around the circle adding ha's until
everyone's stomach hurts from laughing so hard.
It really works. No one can resist Ha Ha—not
even your grumpy neighbor Harold!

All this laughing is bound to make everybody
hungry. See the next page for some easy party
food suggestions.

Quick Tip—Try Some Dip

Here are some food ideas for your next get-together that are really easy to get together. They're all dips!

Dips are perfect party foods because they don't require silverware or plates. And as an extra added advantage, dips give you something to do with your hands while you're standing around talking. (Try gesturing with a celery stick sometime. It's very impressive!)

Big Dippers

First let's talk about the dippers. All of the following foods will taste great with any of the dips (except for the last two dips, which are dessert dips; we'll get to them later).

Pretzels

Breadsticks

Crackers

Melba toast

Potato chips

Corn chips

Carrot sticks

Celery sticks

Raw green beans (soak them in hot water for 15 minutes first)

Raw zucchini (cut into spears or rounds)

Raw cucumber (cut into spears or rounds)

Raw beets (peeled and cut into slices)

Tomatoes (either cherry tomatoes or tomato wedges)

Mushrooms

Scallions

Snow peas (you can eat the shell as well as the peas)

Raw cauliflower (separated into small florets)

Wash all the vegetables well first.

Now—The Dips

Curry in a Hurry

Mix together in a bowl:

2 cups mayonnaise

2 tablespoons curry powder

Keep stirring until the curry is well distributed. Chill for at least an hour. (The dip will turn yellow—it's supposed to.)

Here's a tip: Add the curry one tablespoon at a time. Stir after the first tablespoon and taste. If it tastes strong enough for you, don't add the second tablespoon.

Cool As a Cucumber

Mix together in a bowl:

2 cups sour cream

1 cucumber, chopped into very small pieces

1 teaspoon dried dill or 2 teaspoons chopped fresh dill

Chill and serve.

In the Pink

Mix together in a bowl:

1 cup whipped cream cheese

1 cup sour cream

2 whole pimentos, chopped into tiny pieces

When it's all mixed, sprinkle the top with paprika. Chill and serve.

Thousand Island Dip

Mix together in a bowl:

1 1/2 cups mayonnaise

1/2 cup ketchup

3 tablespoons pickle relish

Chill and serve.

Waldorf Dip

Mix together in a bowl:

2 cups whipped cream cheese

3 tablespoons milk

Mix until the cream cheese is thinned a bit and has a more dippable consistency. Add milk until the consistency is right. Then add:

1/2 cup raisins

1 apple, chopped into small pieces

2 celery stalks, chopped into tiny pieces

Stir, chill, and serve.

Dessert Dips

Use these dippers for dessert dips:
Whole strawberries
Orange slices
Marshmallows
Dried apricots
Apple slices
Peach slices
Banana slices (sprinkle with lemon juice to
  keep them from turning brown)
Vanilla wafers
Doughnut holes
Small squares of sponge cake
Graham crackers

Berry Good Dip
  Mix together in a bowl:
  1 cup strawberry yogurt
  2 cups Cool Whip or other whipped topping
  Chill and serve.

Fun Fondue
  Mix together in a bowl:
  2 cups chocolate syrup
  3 tablespoons orange juice
  Serve as a dip.
  Warning: This is messy. Pass out small plates,
    or you'll be cleaning chocolate syrup off
    the rug for a month!

Try Some New Ways to Say No

You just don't want to go out with the person. But you don't want to hurt his or her feelings. And you don't want to give the usual feeble excuse about having to wash your hair or baby-sit for your little sister.

Well, say *no* to those old excuses—and say *no* with these:

Ten New Excuses for Turning Down a Date

1. I'm sorry, but I don't date anyone from another species.

2. I can't. I promised my parents I'd stay home and annoy my little brother.

3. I have to study. I have a big test coming up in eight or nine weeks.

4. Oh, I'm sorry. I've already made big plans to stay home and watch TV that night.

5. I'm sorry. I don't speak English.

6. I can't. My parents say I'm too old to date. (*That* should confuse 'em!)

7. I'd love to—except that a little green man in a flying saucer is taking me to visit the planet Kar-Zong XII that night. What a pity!

8. Hahahahahahahahahahahaha!

9. I can't. I'm coming down with a bad virus that night.

10. I'm sorry. I can't go out with you. I'm *not* busy that night. (That should *really* confuse 'em!)

Prepare Your Parents— Or Watch Out!

First dates can have their embarrassing moments, as we all know. And if you think you get embarrassed on your own, wait till your parents get into the act!

Face facts—there are certain embarrassing things that parents will *always* say and do whenever a date comes to your house to pick you up. It makes us blush just to think of them!

Perhaps you can head off some of this embarrassment by showing your parents the following list. Let them read it, and keep your fingers crossed. Maybe—just maybe—it will discourage them from saying or doing just a few of these . . .

Things Parents Always Say or Do When Your Date Arrives

Your father will greet your date at the door in hideous red and yellow shorts that are frayed and torn and a T-shirt that says "Plumbers Aren't Always Drips"—and will then make fun of the sports jacket your date is wearing!

Your mother will insist on dragging out the old photo albums and showing your date your baby pictures, and you won't be able to figure out who's more embarrassed—you or him!

No matter how many times you beg and plead with her not to, your mother will immediately ask your date, "What does your father do?"

Your father will insist on telling your date a joke he heard at the office that he thinks is the funniest thing he ever heard. It'll take him twenty minutes to tell the joke—which both of you have already heard a dozen times—and you'll be late for the movie.

Even though your date had a big dinner and politely refuses, your mother will insist on making him try a big portion of her special Lasagne Tutti Frutti Torte Pie.

Your father will say, "Don't walk all the way to the movie. I'll drive you." Then it'll take him half an hour to find his car keys and another half hour to get the car started, and you'll get there just in time to go home.

Your mother will insist on telling your date just how nervous you were before he arrived, how you got nauseous and your stomach growled, and your hands got all cold and clammy because you were so excited.

Your father will insist on talking about how things were different when he was your age.

Your mother will accidentally slip and call you by your baby name (Boo Boo). By Tuesday everyone at school will be calling you Boo Boo.

One or both of your parents will ask your date what he plans to be when he grows up. Then when he says that he doesn't know, it'll get real silent in the room, and no one will know what to say next.

Your father will ask your date to help him change a light bulb in the basement. "It'll only take a second," your father will say. But when your date returns forty-five minutes later, he'll be covered with grease.

Your mother or father will say at least one of the following:

"Don't they look cute together?"

"Don't do anything I wouldn't do! Hahaha!"

"Are you sure you don't want your galoshes?"

"Now, don't get married without calling us and letting us know! Hahaha!"

"Hey—don't be shy. We're just regular folks."

"Remember, kissing spreads germs."

"Don't stay out so late that I'll have to call the police."

"Don't eat too many sweets, dear. Remember how you cried all day about your skin problem."

You and your date will feel like running out of the house screaming!

Get It in Writing

You probably won't want to relive your first dates. But you *will* want to remember them! One good way to keep your memories fresh—and to sum up your feelings about a date—is to keep a written record of the event.

Not everyone has the patience to keep a diary or journal. But here is a fast-to-fill-out record keeper form you might want to use.

Keeping a record of your dating highlights (and lowlights!) can be fun. And when you read it over again months later, your written record may prove to be a lot more entertaining than the original date!

DATE RECORD KEEPER

Name of date:

_____

Date of date:

_____

When and how he/she asked me:

_____

_____

_____

_____

or:

When and how I asked her/him:

_____

_____

_____

_____

Where we went:

_____

_____

_____

_____

What we talked about:

_____

_____

_____

_____

Friends we saw:

_____

_____

_____

_____

Best thing that happened:

_____

_____

_____

_____

Funniest thing that happened:

_____

_____

_____

_____

Least funny thing that happened:

_____

_____

_____

_____

Most embarrassing moment:

_____

_____

_____

_____

I wish I hadn't said:

_____

_____

_____

_____

I'm glad I said:

_____

_____

_____

_____

Thing I'll remember most:

_____

_____

_____

_____

Thing I'd most like to forget:

_____

_____

_____

_____

If I had to describe this date in one word, that word would be:

_____

I give this date a rating of

_____

Instead of 1 to 10, rate your date from A to J!
Use this rating system:

A — absolutely dullsville
B — basically a bomb
C — couldn't be worse
D — don't bring up the subject again!
E — exceptionally mediocre
F — fairly fair
G — good; not great—but good
H — highly enjoyable
I — interesting—*very* interesting!
J — just can't wait till next time!